This book belongs to

....

....

....

For Lili, my little sunshine
For Jeremy

Little Unicorn is
SAD

Aurélie Chien Chow Chine

Buster Books

This is **Little Unicorn**. Most of the time he is just like every other unicorn ... well, almost.

Sometimes **Little Unicorn** is happy.

Sometimes he is unhappy.

Sometimes he is angry.

Sometimes he is sad.

Sometimes he feels sulky.

These are feelings.

And, just like you, **Little Unicorn** has all kinds of feelings.

But **Little Unicorn** has one thing
that makes him magical:

his mane.

When he is having a good day, his mane
twinkles with all the colours of the rainbow.

But when things aren't going well, his mane
changes colour to match how he is feeling.

Happy   Jealous   Angry   Guilty

Shy   Scared   Sulky   Sad

How does **Little Unicorn** feel today?

Bad!

Oh dear. **Little Unicorn** feels bad today.
His heart hurts, like there's a big, grey cloud in it.
He's going to tell us why.

What about you? How do you feel today?

Great

Good

Fine

Not good

Bad

Terrible

Why is **Little Unicorn** feeling sad?

Usually, he is a very happy little unicorn, who loves spending time with his friends, Zachary and Amelia. At school, they often play together at breaktime.

But today, **Little Unicorn** is not
getting along with his friends.

Zachary and Amelia want to play chase,
but **Little Unicorn** wants to play ball.

The friends argue.

Zachary and Amelia go off together to play chase,
leaving **Little Unicorn** all alone with his ball.

Little Unicorn feels sad all day long.

In the evening, **Little Unicorn** is still thinking about the argument with his friends.

He's feeling **sad** and **upset**.

Really, really upset!

It feels like there's a big, grey cloud in his head.
A big cloud full of rain.

What if he used a **breathing exercise**
to chase out that cloud, instead of waiting
for it to go away slowly on its own?

You can do it, too.
When you feel that a cloud of sadness is filling your head,
chase it away with this calming exercise.

A breathing exercise to chase away a cloud of sadness

1 **Little Unicorn** closes his eyes. He imagines
the big, grey cloud in his head.
He breathes through his mouth,
filling up his tummy with air.

2 **Little Unicorn** holds his breath. He pinches his nose shut with his fingers and thinks really hard about the cloud in his head.

3 Then **Little Unicorn** blows all the air out through his nose and chases away the cloud of sadness.

Little Unicorn does this breathing exercise **3 times**.

It takes at least 3 times
to chase away all the raindrops.

After that he can breathe calmly again.

Now that he has chased the cloud out of his head,
he can let the **sunshine** in.

Little Unicorn feels much better and a lot lighter.
He's not cross with his friends any more.

Now that he is feeling good, his mane
is all the colours of the rainbow again.

If you blow the grey cloud away and let
the sunshine in, like **Little Unicorn** did, you will
feel better too. You will feel free as a bird.
And your **smile** will come back!

Edited by Sylvie Michel and Hannah Daffern
Designed by Solène Lavand and cover designed by Angie Allison
Translation by Philippa Wingate

First published in Great Britain in 2019 by Buster Books,
an imprint of Michael O'Mara Books Limited, 9 Lion Yard, Tremadoc Road, London SW4 7NQ

W www.mombooks.com/buster   f Buster Books   🐦 @BusterBooks

ISBN: 978-1-78055-643-7
2 4 6 8 10 9 7 5 3 1

This book was printed in August 2019 by Leo Paper Products Ltd, Heshan Astros Printing Limited,
Xuantan Temple Industrial Zone, Gulao Town, Heshan City, Guangdong Province, China.

Also available:

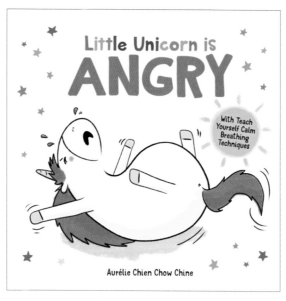

ISBN: 978-1-78055-642-0